❧DECEMBER WITH GOD❧
By ALM Projects

❧ December ☙

This book belongs

Note from the author!

*Show love through love
& mind your own mind- ALM Projects*

Thank you for being part of the *GOD WE TRUST* movement by ALM Projects.

❧Day 1❧

Day

Verse: *And we know that all things work together for good to them that love God, to them who are the called according to his purpose.* **Romans 8:28**

Inspiration: Great is thy faithfulness, Lord unto thee!" I have doubted the Lord's plan for me, having the audacity to demand that He shows me a sign that I can understand. What a fool I have been at times! Look around you: is everything you see, hear, taste, and feel not enough? The Lord is dependable, far more than we are. Strive to be more like Him, more dependable and faithful. It is the greatest gift that we can offer the Lord, and the only one worth giving.

Prayer: Forgive me for losing faith at times, Heavenly Father, for I am weak and foolish at times. I must have tested your patience and am so thankful that your love of me has never waned. Hear me Lord! I am so lucky to be able to love you! It is all that I want to do. I pledge my servitude to you this day and always, Amen.

❧Night❧

Verse: *The people that walked in darkness have seen a great light: they that dwell in the land of the shadow of death, upon them hath the light shined.* **Isaiah 9:2**

Inspiration: Any land without the knowledge of Christ is in deep darkness. And any land that knows about Him but turns away from that knowledge snuffs out its own candle and dooms itself to walk in utter darkness. The Gentile nations were all of them lost in utter heathen darkness, but God sent forth the light of the Gospel all around the world to enlighten their darkness and bring life and hope where there had been none.

Prayer: O Lord Jesus, my life and my heart would be in darkness without you; and my nation would be all darkness, and the whole world complete darkness, without you. Man invents his philosophies and religions which he calls "light," but that is the deepest darkness of all. I praise you that I have seen the true Light and been transformed by it.

Devotion
A prayer for our leaders

This prayer is a blessing for the king and his successor. It is sometimes attributed to Solomon who had himself, asked God for the gift of wisdom. Now the psalm asks that the king be blessed with justice and righteousness. As I read this psalm, I thought of our leaders, most of who are not kings, but have the same responsibilities of ensuring justice for all the people, and helping to bring a sense of peace and security to them. Of course, the one who will bring justice is the Messiah, Jesus. The responsibility for continuing to help bring about justice is also ours. How many times do people worry about how helping others will cost them money! I had a chance to visit a former slave plantation on vacation with my daughter. Our guide was wonderful and I learned quite a bit. He emphasized that the main cause of slavery was greed. Both the owners of slaves and those who had sold their own people into slavery were motivated by greed. Sometimes, those who were sold were people from different tribes that had been captured, but others were from their own people who had the skills that the slave traders were willing to pay for. The owners could get years of work out of the slaves for much less money than if they had paid local workers. But, there are forms of slavery that exist today under different names. There are those who will take girls or boys and get them addicted to drugs so that they can turn them into prostitutes. Still others would not think they were engaging in slavery. These include those businesses that prey upon the poor by paying them "under the table." They receive no benefits and are trapped because they need the money. Other seemingly upright companies will not give their employees enough hours to receive benefits. People will complain about the government having to support the poor, but they will fight a move for businesses to pay a living wage. Where do we stand?

❧Day 2❧

Day
Verse: *And we know that all things work together for good to them that love God, to them who are the called according to his purpose.* **Romans 8:28**

Inspiration: Notice that Paul does not say that all things work together for good for all men generally, but only for those who love God. And note that the grammar is such that "the called" are the same people as "those who love God." And what purpose were they called to? **Verse 29** tells us: to be conformed to the image of His Son.

Prayer: It is easy, Lord; to forget you are working all things together for our good, that you might conform us to the image of Jesus Christ. It is hard for us, sometimes even impossible, to see your purpose in many things that befall us in life. But let us believe your promise and rest on it. Let us not lose heart and faint when faced with trying circumstances.

❧Night❧

Verse: *But he said unto them, Give ye them to eat. And they said, we have no more but five loaves and two fishes; except we should go and buy meat for all his people.* **Luke 9:13**

Inspiration: The disciples saw only the lack of food and of money, but they forgot the power of God. They had seen so many miracles done by Jesus, and yet, they still did not sense the opportunity for God's glory that lay before them. They forgot that "Little is much, if God is in it."

Prayer: Teach us, Lord, to believe in your power and not to despair over our present circumstances. We know you can do great things with very little things. We know you delight to work with what is weak, that your strength might be glorified.

Devotion
Our witness must be faithful

In another place, Jesus will tell the people to listen to the Pharisees but not to act like them. The Pharisees were considered the teachers and upholders of the Jewish traditions. Hopefully, Jesus would not say this about us. We all know the saying, "Do as I say, not as I do." What example do we give others? If we are known as Christians, do our actions proclaim it?

I am aware that we have discussed this question before but it is in line with what we are reading today and we need to reflect on our behavior often. We can't take for granted that we are living as Jesus wants us to live if we don't pay attention. Just as in Lent, we are called to a greater sense of reflection Advent reminds us that this life is not our final home. It can be overwhelming to try to see all of the areas that might need improvement, so I'm suggesting that we take just one of the Ten Commandments that we might have some trouble with and see what changes we need to make to become more faithful to God. Perhaps we have trouble with the truth. Maybe we gossip, wanting to be the first to pass on juicy pieces of information. It might be that we need to clean up our speech and stop swearing and cursing. It can be anything that we find interferes with our relationship with God. If it interferes with our relationships with other people, it interferes with our relationship with God. After all, loving God and loving our neighbor are connected to one another. As John says in his first letter, if we say we love God and hate our neighbor, we are liars. We can't lie to God. We can lie to ourselves, but we cannot lie to God. Let us take this opportunity to prepare ourselves to live eternally with God.

ᔐ**Day 3**ᔑ

Day

Verse: *Thy word is a lamp unto my feet, and a light unto my path.* **Psalm 119:105**

Inspiration: Just as everyone on earth starts from different positions in life, so too our spiritual journey towards the Lord will follow different paths for which there is no set map. There is rather, only the light of the word, and the guidance of the church, but it is still ultimately up to us to take those steps and use what we receive personally, practically, and habitually.

Prayer: I pray for your guidance and light, my Lord, for I am but a lamb in the wilderness without you. When darkness settles down upon me, may you light a path to your loving embrace. When darkness obscures my way, fill my soul with the courage to trust in your holy word. For your testament is the lamp upon my feet, whose flames consume all darkness. Hosanna in the Highest, Amen.

❧Night❧

Verse: *Jesus said unto him, if thou canst believe, all things are possible to him that believeth.* **Mark 9:23**

Inspiration: This father whose son was demon-possessed brought him to Jesus. But while Jesus was away, his disciples were unable to cast out the demon. When Jesus returned, the man said to Jesus "if you can do anything," please have compassion on us. But Jesus answered that "if you can believe, " all things are possible. Then the man cried out "I believe; help my unbelief!"

Prayer: O Author and Finisher of my faith, I believe you but still struggle with unbelief. Help my unbelief, Lord, that I may not question your power to overcome every trial or temptation. You have worked mightily in many others before me, and I know you can do the same for me. Amen.

Devotion
Building our faith on the rock

As we mentioned yesterday, it is important to do what Jesus tells us to do and not just read his words. We need to do the work! Yesterday, I mentioned one way to begin to do the work. Today, I'll mention another. Who do I find difficult to love or forgive? I can name my stumbling blocks; can you name yours? Perhaps it is a family member that just rubs you the wrong way. It might be someone from the past who hurt you and you just can't seem to get past it and forgive. Now, I'm not talking about forgetting because that can put us in danger. After all, we are encouraged to learn from our mistakes, and learning from past relationships that caused us pain can help us to avoid making the same mistakes in the future. But forgiveness enables us to move on, while holding on to anger keeps us stuck in the past. So, how do we begin or continue to build our house of faith on Rock? If we have already been working on love and forgiveness, is there something else we need to do? Maybe we need to be better at looking at all the good things God has done for us and work on developing a better sense of gratitude instead of taking these gifts for granted.   Maybe we need to reread the Beatitudes and see if we are merciful or peacemakers.   I'm sure that if we ask God, God will guide us to the next rock to place on our foundation to fortify it so that we may stand secure in the face of temptation or trouble.

❧Day 4❧

Day

Verse: *Have not I commanded thee? Be strong and of a good courage; be not afraid, neither be thou dismayed: for the LORD thy God is with thee whithersoever thou go.* **Joshua 1:9**

Inspiration: At the start of the book of Joshua, Moses has died and there is a feeling of fear in all of the Israelites. God commands Joshua to not be afraid, to trust in Him, because the Lord will always be with Him. Although it might not feel so direct or clear, God has done the same for all of us, by sending His son to earth to live, die, and reborn for us. So go out to love the Lord and the people, serve the Lord and the people. Leave everything we own to our one true Lord!

Prayer: Abba Father, You stand with us even when it seems that we are alone. Give me the courage to stand up and hate evil, to not feel discouraged in dark times, and to be faithful even when others' faith wavers. It is only through you that I will find the way, the truth, and the life. I submit myself totally to ye, wondrous God, and it is in your name that I pray, Amen.

❧Night❧

Verse: *Search for the verse and write down.*

____

____

____

Leviticus 10:3

Inspiration: Aaron's sons had offered "strange fire," unauthorized incense, before Jehovah-God and had been consumed by the fire of God before the people of Israel. We are not to worship God in any way we please but according to the manner he has prescribed. We are to keep the worship of God holy, not intermix it with the ways of the world.

Prayer: Help me to worship you aright, O God. Teach my heart to hallow your holy name. Teach my lips to praise you according to truth. Teach my hands to work for your glory and my feet to go where you send me. Make all my life an act of worship of you, O Lord.

Below write your own prayer!

____

____

____

Devotion
God will guide us

We do not need to do all the work alone. God is there to show us the way. All we have to do is ask. One summer, I was very afraid. My job had ended and I had five children to feed, clothe and house. I had found a temporary position but it was way out of my field and sitting at a desk all day for little money was a necessity but not what I needed. I had applied for a teaching position for which I was qualified – unlike the other position! Before I got a response from the school, the company where I was working offered me a permanent position. I was in a bind and didn't know what I should do. God needed to help me, and quickly! The above psalm was my prayer: show me the way! Before the deadline to accept or reject the office position, I received an answer that I had been accepted for the teaching position. I cannot even now express accurately how much I was grateful to God for his guidance. So many times we can be tempted to go our own way without checking with God if this is the right way to go. When we do, we can be surprised by the answers we get. Sometimes it's hard to wait for the Lord, but the rewards are great. Where do you need the Lord to direct your ways this Advent? Where will we find truth? Are we open to his teaching? All are questions we need to ask ourselves as we prepare for Christmas.

❧Day 5❧

Day

Verse*: Have not I commanded thee? Be strong and of a good courage; be not afraid, neither be thou dismayed: for the LORD thy God is with thee whithersoever thou goes.* **Joshua 1:9**

Inspiration: Fear is one of the number one things holding people back from living happier and more productive lives. Fear of harm, fear of responsibility, but perhaps most insidiously, fear of rejection from others. Yet, with God as our Light and our ultimate redeemer, there is resolutely nothing to fear, for nothing can overpower God's will. So long as we are disciples of His word, He cannot, and will not, turn His back on us.

Prayers: Lord, within the darkest depths of my soul, dispels my fears with your light! Grant me courage in the face of all adversity, knowing that you are my armor. Let me not be dismayed, for in living in your name, I need not know fear or rejection. For in you all things are possible. By Your grace grant me this, at once by my side and within my heart, Amen.

❧Night❧

Verse: *And the children of Israel said unto the LORD, We have sinned: do thou unto us whatsoever seemed good unto thee; deliver us only, we pray thee, this day*: **Judge 10:15**

Inspiration: Here is the repeated cry of Israel again and again in the Book of Judges. They would serve the LORD for a time, depart from him to go after idols, then judgment would fall on them, then they would cry out to the LORD for help, and he would rise up a judge to deliver them. This cycle can mirror our struggles in the Christian life as well, but far better when we simply consistently follow God.

Prayer: O ever-present Helper of my soul, if I have sinned, I turn to you to forgive me and deliver me. There is no one else to whom I can turn for help, nor am I able to fight the good fight of faith alone. I confess and forsake my sins by your grace, leave me not to drift in my own direction.

Devotion
They need good shepherds

I wonder what Jesus is thinking about our world today. We certainly are scattered and at times are harassed for our faith. The world bombards us with messages contrary to the word of God. Who do we allow to shepherd us?   Do we look to the Lord for guidance?   There are many good ministers and priests today who share the Good News of the Kingdom, but their voices are often silenced by those who would have us go the other way. We were given the job of protecting our world by God in Genesis. Religious leaders tell us that we need to protect the environment and not be wasteful, but others tell us that progress is more important. I don't think that those who live with polluted air and undrinkable water would agree! Again, justice for the poor is a major theme of both the Old and New Testaments as it exemplifies the law of love. But justice for whom? There are those who believe that some are more entitled to "justice" than others. One example of this is the disproportionate numbers of the poor or those of color in the prison system in the United States. In other countries, the laws are in favor of men and do not protect the rights of women and girls. At times, Scripture is even used to justify the actions of those who are in power. Who are the shepherds? Where can we hear their voices? Jesus sent out the apostles and disciples to help shepherd the people of his time. Now we have been sent by virtue of our Baptism to help shepherd the people of our time. If we are to fulfill this responsibility, then we need to keep close to The Shepherd by listening to his voice and following him.

❧Day 6❧

Day

Verse: For the grace of God that brings salvation hath appeared to all men, Teaching us that, denying ungodliness and worldly lusts, we should live soberly, righteously, and godly, in this present world; **Titus 2:11-12**

Inspiration: The instructions are simple, but to follow them is not easy. The present world is filled with temptations and sin. Luckily we are all given a CHOICE, how to live, given to us only through the salvation through the grace of God. Realize and refuse these temptations and we can appreciate the sacrifice made to save mankind.

Prayer: Heavenly Father, what you ask of us is simple yet easy to forget. Help lead us away from the sin and evils of this world. Lead us towards a life of righteousness and faith. A life worth living is one that follows your word. It is the only way, the truth and the light. Pray all of this in your holy name. Amen.

❧Night❧

Verse: Not forsaking the assembling of ourselves together, as the manner of some is; but exhorting one another: and so much the more, as ye see the day approaching. **Hebrew 10:25**

Inspiration: While we can have fellowship with God and with other Christians at other places than at church, God has established churches for our edification and growth in godliness. He commands us not to forsake to attend them in favor of merely watching preachers on TV or hearing no preaching of the Word at all.

Prayer: Give me, O Lord, a strong desire to fellowship with your people and learn from your Word at a local Church that I can regularly attend. Help me to find the time and resources to attend it. Help me to consistently attend unless there be a valid reason why I'm unable to for a particular day. I love your people, O Lord, and desire a regular "church home."

Devotion
The Gifts of the spirit

So many of Isaiah's prophesies look forward to the coming of the Messiah! It is no wonder that we read so many of them during Advent and

Lent. In today's passage, we read not only the virtues that the Messiah will possess, but also the gifts that we are given by the Holy Spirit. If you were to ask for just one of them today, which would it be? As I write this, I am preparing for a trip with one of my daughters to visit her daughter, my granddaughter, who lives more than fifteen hundred miles away. I think I would ask for a spirit of counsel, right judgment. There are so many things that can come up on so long a trip. Most of it will be in the air, but there are unknowns driving around a strange city, walking unfamiliar streets and making choices as to how to spend our time. I have been there before, but there have been some severe storms in the area, and I don't know what challenges I might face. There are times when I most needed wisdom, and other times when I needed understanding. It can be hard to know what another person is going through, and we need to know when compassion is called for and when we need to give tough love. When are we showing mercy, and when are we enabling destructive behavior? Although it is not our job to judge, we are often called to make the right decision as how to help. Our lives take different turns each day and our situation may call for one of another of these gifts. What we need to remember is that all we have to do is ask, and God will answer.

❧Day 7☙

Day

Verse: *Looking for that blessed hope, and the glorious appearing of the great God and our Savior Jesus Christ; Who gave himself for us, that he might redeem us from all iniquity, and purify unto himself a peculiar people, zealous of good works.* **Titus 2:13-14**

Inspiration: Even amidst the harshest environments, seeds may produce flowers of life. Churches may often seem like these places, scrunched in between the most hostile of environments or towering metropolises. The real temple of God is within our hearts if needs be our places of worship could be as simple as a room with a few chairs. Our zealotry, our love of Christ and the gospel are what allow us to survive in some of these places. So praise be to the Lord! For Him we will forever endure!

Prayer: Lord my guide, my Heavenly Father and light within the desert or the storm, grant to all your children a life of joy and worship within Your Temple. For whether in Heaven or on earth, our hearts labor for only You Lord, who can deliver us from death and forever grant us grace. Amen.

❧Night❧

Verse: *Riches profit not in the day of wrath: but righteousness delivered from death.* **Proverbs 11:4**

Inspiration: Many may heap up earthly treasures and trust in them to deliver them, but even with mere men, money cannot always avail. Not all judges will take a bribe, and no gift will pacify those who have been deeply offended and severely misused. How much less can money avail anything at all on the day of God's holy wrath!

Prayer: Lord, though a man gains all the money in the world, he could not buy salvation from you. Your anger against sin cannot be appeased by any riches that men might try to offer, and the offer itself would insult your holiness. Nor can good works, long prayers, or self-affliction avail anything. It is only the blood of your Son Jesus Christ that can quench the fire of your wrath. In that alone I ever trust.

Devotion
God comes to save us

During the season of Advent we look to Isaiah more than the other prophets for inspiration. The Israelites needed encouragement as they watched their land be overtaken, their people either killed or sent into exile and the temple in Jerusalem looted and destroyed. This is one of the prophesies that give the people hope that God will come and save them, but also is used as a reference to the coming of the Messiah. We also need hope when life is difficult because of sickness or tragedy. We need the assurance that God is in control and will come and save us. As I write this, there is a hurricane damaging islands in the Caribbean that haven't yet recovered from damage suffered a few years ago. People, who had little before, will lose even more now and some will lose everything. Many of these people have a firm faith in God that sustained them in the past and, hopefully, will sustain them again. If not hurricanes, then earthquakes or forest fires, floods or tornadoes may come and destroy both lives and properties and test people's faith. It's hard to hang on when you see your life's work disappear before your eyes. It only by believes in the promises of Jesus that we can survive what life throws at us. We need to have our knees strengthened along with our fearful hearts. We don't know God's plan any more than the Israelites did, and there are times when we can even question God's wisdom. I'm sure that the Israelites kept waiting for relief just as we often do. For the Israelites it would take several lifetimes for God's promise to be fulfilled. For us, it can seem like that, but we know that

the Messiah has come; that we have
been saved, and we will see the glory
of God in heaven.

✋Day 8✋

Day
Verse: And not only they, but ourselves also, which have the first fruits of the Spirit, even we ourselves groan within ourselves, waiting for the adoption, to wit, the redemption of our body. **Romans 8:23**

Inspiration: Though Christians have received the new nature, they are not yet fully changed. And our bodies are not changing at all at present, but are growing old like those of anyone else. But we groan for deliverance from sin and look forward to the day when we will be free from the hindrances and limitations of our present weak bodies.
Prayer

We wait, O Lord, for the day when you will complete the work You began in us. We walk by faith and not by sight. You have left us for now in these fragile "jars of clay" with your glory hidden inside, that men may see that the power is all of You and not of us. But we rejoice that You will glorify Your saints and believe in the resurrection.

❧Night❧

Verse: *And no marvel; for Satan himself is transformed into an angel of light.* **2 Corinthians 11:14**
Inspiration

For the most part, those spreading doctrines of devils and lies hatched by Satan do not openly reveal their true identity, and many do not even know they are being used as Satan's dupe. Satan tries to present his false doctrines as good in order to gain wider acceptance. Therefore, we cannot judge by appearances but must judge by the standard of revealed truth from God.

Prayer: O Giver of truth, give us discernment through your Word and Spirit. Let us not fall prey to deceptions of Satan or his henchmen. Let us not be naive, but let us realize that wolves often cover themselves with sheepskins and Satan likes to disguise himself as an angel of light. We know you will save us from Satan's devices, for greater is he who is in us than he who is in the world.

Devotion
God has done great things for us

Mary has just told the angel Gabriel that she is willing to become the mother of Jesus and has gone to visit her cousin Elizabeth who is pregnant with John the Baptist. Mary's response is the prayer called "The Magnificent." Elizabeth was praising Mary for saying "yes" to the angel and Mary knows that she has been chosen for a very important mission and feels her own unworthiness. Do we ever think about the fact that we are also chosen, though unworthy, to do God's work? If we are made in God's image, and have received the Holy Spirit in Baptism, then we too are called to "magnify" the Lord in our daily lives. We too are blessed by God. God has done great things for us in giving us the gift of faith. This gift allows us to be adopted children of the one God, heirs to the Kingdom earned for us by Jesus. We too should be grateful for all that God has done for us and praise God who is holy just as Mary does in this passage from Luke. During this season of Advent, we should also thank Mary for agreeing to be the mother of our Savior. Have you ever considered what would have happened if she had said "no?" My imagination sometimes goes off on those tangents. I have often wondered if Abraham had been the first person that God approached. And I have wondered the same about Mary. The same applies to us. Why do we have the gift of faith, and not others? As for me, I am grateful to God and I feel very blessed that I have a faith that gets me through the highs and lows of life with a promise of eternal life when this one on earth ends.

❧Day 9❧

Day

Verse: *The LORD is nigh unto them that are of a broken heart; and saves such as be of a contrite spirit.* **Psalm 34:18**

Inspiration: You will experience loss and betrayal. There will be times when you feel brokenhearted. We live in a fallen world, so it is expected that we will experience pain and hurt. However, those who believe in the Lord will find relief in him. The Bible tells us He is close to those who are brokenhearted and He saves those who feel crushed in spirit. When you are hurting, call out to Jesus. He is always faithful and He will give you peace.

Prayer: Dear God, I am brokenhearted. I am overwhelmed with sadness. You understand pain as your son suffered on the cross – be near me, O Lord. But, Father, I know I can call on you and you will give me peace and rest. You see my pain and you will give me the strength I need to overcome this trial. Turn my mourning into gladness, Lord. In Jesus' name, amen.

❧Night❧

Verse: *For he was a good man, and full of the Holy Ghost and of faith: and much people was added unto the Lord.* **Acts 11:24**

Inspiration: Barnabus was so trusted as to be sent by the Jerusalem Church to investigate the reports of Gentile converts in Antioch. He rejoiced in what he found God had done, and through him, many more were added to the Church. Barnabus was full of the Holy Spirit, meaning submissive to Him in his daily walk, which led to his being used greatly of God.

Prayer: Use me, Lord, as you used Barnabus, to lead many to you, I pray. Help me submit to the Spirit's leading, which comes through your Word, that I may be ready to speak and act for you in every situation that arises.

Devotion
Jesus will help us carry our burdens

Jesus wants us to be free of the burdens we carry. There's a story about a man who has many responsibilities at work and they often cause him concern. He also has a family at home and he has chosen not to be a burden to them. When asked by a friend how he manages, he tells them that he leaves his work concerns in the tree at the end of the walkway to his home and doesn't pick them up until the next morning on his way to work. Now, Jesus wants us to give him our burdens and not pick them back up! There's a familiar saying, "Let go and let God." I know this is easier said than done, but it is what God wants. What is the yoke of Christ? We find rest for our souls in the love and promises of Christ. The burden we then pick up is the burden to love, to be gentle with ourselves and with others. The more we let Jesus carry our daily burdens trusting him to guide us and help us deal with them, the easier it is to be restful and gentle with ourselves. We somehow have gotten the world's message that we have to do it all; be it all. Women are told that being a wife and mother is not enough; they need to make their mark on the business world as well. Men are told that they can't have compassion for others, but must hold in all their emotions and be strong! Parents can be expected to put themselves into debt to educate their children. Even children can bear the burden of proving themselves to parents or friends. Burdens! No one can do everything especially if they think it all has to be done yesterday and alone! God is here. We need to slow down, take Jesus' advice, and let him help with whatever burden we think we need to carry alone.

❧Day 10❧

Day

Verse: *Blessed be God, even the Father of our Lord Jesus Christ, the Father of mercies, and the God of all comfort; Who comforted us in all our tribulation, that we may be able to comfort them which are in any trouble, by the comfort wherewith we ourselves are comforted of God.* **2 Corinthians 1:3-4**

Inspiration: Good friends and family members have comforted me more times than I can remember when times were tough. My best friends comforted me without me even asking, seemingly knowing when I needed to be comforted. This is the way of the Holy Spirit, flowing through all of us to others in need. Submit it to the Spirit!

Be comforted by it and comfort others with it! Praise be to the Father, Son, and Holy Spirit!

Prayer: Precious God, the Holy Spirit binds all Christians together. Christ's compassion taught us how to be comforted and how to comfort others, and I pray that you utilize my gifts to comfort others, gracious Lord! I ask that the next time someone around me needs to be comforted, you move me with the Spirit to positively touch them. I pray this in the name of the Father of compassion, Jesus Christ. Amen.

❧Night❧

Verse: *And ye have forgotten the exhortation which speaks unto you as unto children, my son, despise not thou the chastening of the Lord, nor faint*

when thou art rebuked of him:
Hebrew 3:5

Inspiration: Even as an earthly father who loves his children will chastise (discipline) them if he truly loves them and wants what is best for them, so also is our Heavenly Father. He does not condemn us like a judge in a courtroom, for there is no condemnation to those in Christ. His punishments of us are not legal, but parental. They are not required by "the rules," but are done as needed to help us grow and learn his ways of holiness for our good and his glory.

Prayer: Let me not resent your discipline, O Father, for I know that if you discipline me, it is only because you love me. Help me to want what you want for me, to desire the object of your discipline, which is to teach me you're word and lead me in the paths of righteousness for your name's sake. Amen.

Devotion
Tell the children of the glory of God

This is a good time to stop in our Advent preparations to make sure that we are passing on to future generations the goodness of God and his wondrous deeds. Have we already begun telling our children the story of Christmas from Luke's Gospel? After all, the media is already telling them the story of Santa Claus, Rudolph, Frosty the Snowman and any number of movies that have nothing to do with Jesus! We are the generation that is responsible for declaring God's mighty act to the next generation and if not us, then who? Are we still taking time to reflect on how our behavior is witnessing our faith? If not, we're only a third of the way through Advent so we still have time. That changes have we made? Are we kinder, more compassionate, and forgiving? Are we truly praising God every day? We declare that we are followers of Jesus, but are we sure that the path we are on is the one he wants us to be on? This is a tough time. There are so many distractions. If you work in retail, you are probably working overtime and are stressed because you don't have time to do your own shopping. I remember the days when I needed to work right up to the last minute. So, instead of stressing, I would pile the kids in the car, let the older ones pick up something for the grandparents, while I took the youngest and bought everything I needed to get all at once. Of course, I didn't have much money, so I could only get one or two things each. I can't see the point of going into debt for birthdays or holidays. Take some time today to breathe in the love of Christ and prepare the gift you are going to give him for his birthday.

❧Day 11☙

Day

Verse: *And the Lord make you to increase and abound in love one toward another, and toward all men, even as we do toward you:* **1 Thessalonians 3:12**

Inspiration: As we follow God's guidance in our lives, we will express more and more of His nature in our daily lives. We will become more understanding towards our fellow brothers and sisters in Christ and this will help us forgive and love one another wholeheartedly. As we grow in our love for one another, our testimony of Jesus Christ will become more effective and powerful because we will not just be giving the world our words, we will be backing up our words with action as well.

Prayer: Dear God, I pray for the collective body of Christ across the world. Lord, I pray that the love we have for one another will grow day by day. May we all be attentive to your guidance, Father, especially when it comes to how we fellowship with one another so that our actions will always be based on love and nothing else. May the love we have for one another be a testimony to the world of Your goodness and Your love, Father. In Jesus' name, I pray. Amen.

❧Night❧

Verse: *Recompense to no man evil for evil. Provide things honest in the sight of all men. If it be possible, as much as* *lies in you, live peaceably with all men.* **Romans 12:17-18**

Inspiration: It is not always possible to live for God and to live at peace with all men. But insofar as it is possible, we should strive to do so. We should never delight in conflict and controversy for its own sake but only engage in such when necessary and to defend the truth and live the truth. Christians should be characterized as "people of peace" who are willing to "get along with" others as long as that does not entail denying their God.

Prayer

You, Lord, have reconciled us to yourself, giving us your peace. And we know that in the world we shall have tribulation. But let us not be such as refuse to live in peace with others and create needless conflicts. Let our desire for peace with others be a testimony to them of a Spirit-led attitude.

Devotion
By what standards do we judge?

There's just no pleasing some people! Jesus is talking about the leaders' reaction to both John the Baptist and himself. When John came preaching a message of repentance so as to prepare for the coming Messiah, people began to come to him to be baptized. This didn't make the Jewish leaders happy and so they complained. Jesus came along, preaching the Good News of salvation and they were even more upset. They compared his behavior to John's and complained again, even stating that John's disciples obeyed the law more than the disciples of Jesus. I guess they forgot that they shouldn't judge. We often do the same thing.   Sometimes we even pass judgment on the same person – twice! We might have a friend or relative who has gotten into trouble. It could be something illegal or it could be an addiction that is out of control. We judge them, not their behavior, and decide to turn our backs on them. Then, they clean up their act, pay for their past behavior, stop using whatever they have become addicted to. Do we welcome them back into our lives? Some might, but others will say that it's all an act and they are still not worthy of our love. This has happened to well-known figures in the media or sports as well. One mistake and that's it! Judge not lest you be judged is not part of the make-up of some people. Again, I'm not saying that we should leave money hanging around if someone has had a problem with theft or gambling, or that we should offer an alcoholic a drink once they have achieved sobriety, but we should look at the person and give them a chance. Both John the Baptist and Jesus were judged unfairly, we need to be careful not to fall into the same trap.

❧Day 12❧

Day

Verse: *For God hath not given us the spirit of fear; but of power, and of love, and of a sound mind.* **2 Timothy 1:7**

Inspiration: Human life is fragile, frail, finite, and natural. God's strength is awesome, incomprehensible, infinite, and supernatural. The Holy "Spirit is love, joy, peace, longsuffering, gentleness, goodness, faith, Meekness, temperance." **(Galatians 5: 22-23).** It is strong yet gentle, filled with love and asks nothing of us. "How much more shall your heavenly Father give the Holy Spirit to them that ask him?"**(Luke 11:13)**

Prayer: I am weary, Lord. I pray to you today, my rock and redeemer, asking that You catch me when I run to You. I know that you will be the wind beneath my wings, so that I will be like an eagle, soaring into the heavens. My eyes are solely on you, and I pray that You will work through me and others. Thank you for all that You have given me, benevolent God and Abba Father! I love you with all of my heart and strength, Amen.

❧Night❧

Verse: *Now ye are the body of Christ, and members in particular.* **1 Corinthians 12:27**

Inspiration: Of every true church it can be said, "you are the Body of Christ, the Bride of Christ, the people of God, the children of God, the saints of God, the Church of God. " And of every true Christian, it can be said, you are a member of these groups, which are one and the same group really but under different names.

Prayer: Lord, there are many members but one Body. And if each local church is "a body of Christ, " there is still that bigger, single, all-encompassing "the Body of Christ. " There is a mystical union among all believers of all time and in all places who have been placed in union with your Son. May I fellowship freely with all true sons of God that I meet and rejoice to see the work you have done in their lives.

Devotion
The path to God is the path to peace

If we want peace, then we need to listen to the voice of God and pay attention to living out the commandments. This is not new; it is as old as the first covenant. The Israelites failed to obey and they lost their lands and the temple. It took an outsider, Cyrus, to restore the remnant of Israel to Jerusalem and rebuild the temple. The people of Jesus' time didn't listen to his voice and again Jerusalem was lost and the temple destroyed. We don't know what will happen today if we don't listen and obey. We do know that the world is not at peace. Although we are not suffering a world-wide war, there is war going on in every corner of the world and there is violence everywhere. Peace does not reign. We are once again preparing to celebrate the birth of the King of Peace. But unless we listen to his voice, we will not have peace. Just like the Israelites who turned to idols thinking that they would save them, we often turn to idols ignoring the One who has the ability to save us from ourselves. Without peace in our hearts, we won't have peace in the world. Hearts that are controlled by sinfulness are not at peace. The liar is always worried that they will be found out. The greedy will never be satisfied with what they have. The proud will be afraid that someone might figure out that they really don't know everything. Anger is both self-destructive and dangerous for those around us. If we truly want peace, let us concentrate on being peaceful people. This is the perfect time to start.

❧Day 13❧

Day

Verse: *For what the law could not do, in that it was weak through the flesh, God sending his own Son in the likeness of sinful flesh, and for sin, condemned sin in the flesh: That the righteousness of the law might be fulfilled in us, who walk not after the flesh, but after the Spirit.* **Romans 8:3-4**

Inspiration: Paul tells us that the Law of God was "weak" due to the "flesh." This is to say that the Law's function was only to be light, revealing to us the moral will of God and revealing to us our own sinfulness and need of a Savior. In its purpose, the Law is powerful, but it is "weak" in that it cannot save and sanctify in and of itself.

Prayer: Lord, we know that the law could not save, could not enable us to keep your commands. Law can only tell us what we ought to do, and does nothing more than that. The righteousness of the Law is fulfilled in us, your children, because of your transforming power. We long for your righteousness and pursue it. And we know that you will fulfill all of your purposes for us.

❧Night❧

Verse: *Be not forgetful to entertain strangers: for thereby some have entertained angels unawares.* **Hebrew 13:2**

Inspiration: We should always be mindful of the people we come across in our lives. Whether they share the same beliefs as us, we should never treat someone badly. As Christians, we should allow the love in our hearts to lead us in treating everyone warmly. In times of the Old Testament, people would entertain guests and some of those guests turned out to be angels. Be kind to everyone you come across – angel or not. It's the best way to express the love of God within us.

Prayer: Dear God, I pray that I will love and accommodating to every person I come across – regardless of the differences we may share. Lord, may I reflect your love in the way I treat my brothers and sisters in the Lord, and those who may not know you. When I come across strangers, may my heart be welcoming towards them. In Jesus' name, I pray. Amen.

Devotion

Patience is important but difficult in today's world. We have come to expect instant results in so many areas of life. The farmer, the gardener, and the craftsman all understand the need for patience. You can't hurry the weather, or control the sunshine, and work done by hand is painstaking and slow. However, we have instant replays of sports games; we use microwaves and instant pots to cook meals in minutes. Cars go faster and faster, and computers give us information almost faster than we can type the questions. James is letting the early Christians know that they, too, must have patience as they await Jesus' coming back in glory. Just like them, we need patience. To me this says that we need to live each day as if he is coming soon, and keep living as Jesus wants us to even if it means we will spend years doing so. In the long run, it doesn't matter whether or not Jesus returns during our lifetime. We will be judged at the time of our death. We don't want to be found unworthy. I never worry about the end of the world for this reason. I only need to be concerned with my end! The way we live each day, the choices we make to live as Jesus calls us to live, the way we work for justice, will determine whether we spend eternity in the kingdom or not. The kingdom of the Lord is at hand for each of us even though we don't know the day or the hour. Let us work each day to be prepared to meet Jesus when he comes for us.

❦Day 14❦

Day

Verse: *Him that is weak in the faith receive ye, but not to doubtful disputations.* **Romans 14:1**

Inspiration: To those newly admitted to our faith, we should give extra attention and care to. Like a new hatchling, they require nurturing, instruction and help. We do this not only because it is our duty, but because we would hope the same welcoming hand would be extended to us if it were the other way around. Soon, they will be able to fly by themselves. And who knows, maybe they would end up soaring to the highest of heights? What better way to please God than to have had a hand in having helped another reach the Promised Land?

Prayer: My Lord, grant me the guidance and patience you have shown me to those who are only now hearing your name and wish to know your truth. Grant me patience and care, so that I may help serve you by serving them. For my wish is only to please you my Lord, and do your work by helping bring your children into the light.

❧Night❧

Verse: *Rejoice not in iniquity, but rejoice in the truth;* **1 Corinthians 13:6**

Inspiration: There is never a time or an excuse for rejoicing in iniquity. We must always flee from immorality and never let it become a part of our lives. When we are in places where immorality is rife, we should take our stand as believers on the word of God. This does not mean we need to be harsh against anyone, no. It is possible to love sinners and evildoers without tolerating their actions. God gives us wisdom to do so.

Prayer: Dear God, I thank you for your wisdom that enables me to never tolerate or make excuses for immorality. Father, if I am ever in a situation where people rejoice in practicing immorality, may you give me the courage to speak up and the wisdom to say the right words. In Jesus' name, I pray. Amen.

Devotion
Open my eyes to see you

We are more than halfway through Advent, and as often as I have read the Bible, and as often as I have read the scriptures suggested for

Advent, this is the first time I have actually paid attention to this reading from Numbers. Balaam is mentioned in the second letter of Peter as a man who loved being paid for wrongdoing but was stopped on his journey by an angel who appeared to him. However, he did not see the angel, but his ass did. Only because God allowed his ass to speak, were Balaam's eyes opened to see the angel. Those who were waiting for Balaam wanted him to curse the Israelites, but God only allowed him to speak God's words. After three tries to get him to do what they wanted him to do, they let him go and Balaam returned to the camp. Although this passage is not mentioned anywhere in the New Testament, it is considered a Messianic prophecy. It is thought that the Messiah is the star that will come out of Jacob and the scepter that will rise out of Israel. I'm sure that this is why it is included in the Advent readings. In reading about Balaam and his oracles, it made me wonder how often our eyes are closed to the actions of God and what must it take for us to finally see. I doubt that we will have an animal speak to us to let us know what God wants us to do, but I do believe that he sends people into our lives to open our eyes and wake us up to the presence of God in our lives. I know that there have been times when a chance meeting or a brief conversation has stopped me in my tracks and made me reexamine what I thought I knew. We always need to be open to see and hear the messages God wants us to know, or that God wants us to share with others.

❧Day 15❧

Day

Verse: *Now unto him that is able to do exceeding abundantly above all that we ask or think, according to the power that worked in us, unto him be glory in the church by Christ Jesus throughout all ages, world without end. Amen.* **Ephesians 3:20-21**

Inspiration: There is an ancient Latin expression first recorded by Pliny the Elder, where a famous painter asked a local shoemaker to give instructions on a new painting, specifically in the artists' rendering of a sandal. Duly, the shoemaker made his critique, and the mistake was rectified. Encouraged by his new found power, the shoemaker started critiquing other things in the painting, offering his opinions blindly.

Seeking an end to this, in divulging his thoughts on things he was perhaps ignorant of, the painter replied: "Shoe maker, do not look beyond the foot [Suttor, ne ultra crepidam]". This anecdote may illustrate the point that no matter how powerful, successful or rich, no matter how confident we may feel in ourselves and our own abilities, we are but lowly children still in comparison to our Lord Almighty, whose power we only understand a fraction of. We are not the ultimate masters of our destiny, rather it is God who decides, who determines our fates, sometimes above our own understanding.

Prayer: Lord God, the most almighty! Above our power and into the internal paradise, you see all we do and are capable of. I thank you for all You have given me O Lord, and pray that even with these abundant gifts I may stay humble within Your presence. For above us, is Your divine plan, and wrong are we to try and deny its unfolding, erred are we to try and deny Your higher power that works within us. Praise be Your name, Amen.

❧Night❧

Verse: *My son, let not them depart from your eyes: keep sound wisdom and discretion: So shall they be life unto thy soul, and grace to thy neck.* **Proverbs 3:21-22**

Inspiration: We should keep wisdom – godly wisdom – and discretion close to our hearts. The world is full of devices of deception; as Christians, we have to stay alert. God's wisdom shows us the way to go and all the things to turn away from and avoid.

We will find life in God's counsel and nowhere else; we must cling to it, never wanting to let go.

Prayer: Dear God, may I always desire to hear and be attentive to your wisdom. Lord, I am aware that this world is full of deception, but you have equipped me with the wisdom to overcome all traps. Father, may I always seek you for discernment in all situations. In Jesus' name, I pray. Amen.

Devotion
Doing God's will is more important than promising to do

In the parable of the two sons, we see something that is played out every day in our homes, our work places and in the public arena. The first son is quick to promise to do something for his father, but doesn't follow through, but the second son has a change of heart after refusing his father's request and does the will of his father. On the theological side, we understand that Jesus is speaking to a crowd who believe that, as the Chosen People of God, they are guaranteed a place in the kingdom, but that sinners and Gentiles will not be allowed in. But if we only reflect on this interpretation, we may miss the point for ourselves. We too may have minds that are closed to the reality that Jesus came to save everyone. There is a joke that ends with the name of each denomination in heaven believing that they are the only ones there, so St. Peter requests that the newly admitted to the kingdom tiptoe past their closed doors so as not to spoil their day. No one of us is guaranteed eternal life with God in heaven even though each one of us is promised eternal life. We are called to respond to God's promise by the way in which we live – with love, justice, forgiveness, compassion, in other words, doing the will of the Father. Now some of us will have periods of rebellion – just like teenagers in a family – but the important thing is to have a change of heart, a conversion, and bring our lives back on track. It's not enough to SAY we believe, we need to DO the will of our Father.

❧Day 16❧

Day

Verse: *For unto you it is given in the behalf of Christ, not only to believe on him, but also to suffer for his sake;*

Inspiration: Have you heard the phrase, "What doesn't kill you makes you stronger?" Suffering and pain are things that humans naturally avoid. It is in our most basic instinct to avoid these things in order to survive. Pain and suffering in the name of Jesus Christ do make you stronger: to be more faithful, more loving, and to be saved. Longsuffering is an often mentioned virtue in the Bible. Suffering in the name of Jesus builds patience and helps you gain perspective. Pain and suffering help believes in Christ sympathize with what He went through for us. Withstand it on behalf of Christ and you will be stronger.

Prayer: Gracious and beautiful God, my Abba Father, I ask for you in my hour of suffering. Sustain me with my power, to overcome any worldly pain that I may endure. I know that through You I can withstand all temptation and any suffering is a privilege in the name of Jesus Christ. I shall devote my life to your service Lord, and it is in your name I pray. Amen.

❧Night❧

Verse: *He that dwelled in the secret place of the most high shall abide under the shadow of the Almighty.* **Psalm 9:11**

Inspiration: The secret place of the Most High God is found in Jesus Christ. To the men of the old, the plan of Christ to come was a mystery. But we, who are in the new covenant, no longer behold mysteries because God has revealed everything to us. We dwell in Christ and in Him we are protected from the devices of the enemy.

Prayer: Dear God, I thank you for the security that I have in Christ. Though the enemy may try to bring me down, I know that he will never succeed because I am hidden in you, Lord. May I never lose hope, Lord, and may I always remember the great assurance I have in you. In Jesus' name, I pray. Amen.

Devotion
God is good and there is no other

"I am God, and there is no other." That means that I am not a god, sports is not, wealth is not, fame is not. However, we know that all of these can be a idols that people worship. The Israelites were worshiping idols, bowing to the altars of sacrifice to Baal, and making alliances that they believed would save them. They didn't listen to Isaiah. They were overcome and sent into exile. At this point in the Book of Isaiah, they are back in Israel after years of exile thanks to Cyrus who acted on behalf of the God of Israel. God had saved them and brought them home. Now they have a second chance to bow only before God. We know that they will fail again. However, this passage is here during Advent to point also to Jesus, as Son of God who will save all of us and open the gates to heaven. If you think some of these phrases sound familiar, you are correct. In the hymn included in Paul's letter to the Philippians, chapter 2, we read, "that at the name of Jesus every knee should bow, of those in heaven those of earth, and those under the earth and that every tongue should confess that Jesus Christ is Lord, to the glory of God the Father." This is not a coincidence. The early Christians believed, as we do that Jesus was divine as well as human. Many of them had been witnesses to the resurrection and saw that those who had "raged against" Jesus to the point of crucifixion were not only disappointed, but furious that they had been unable to stop the Good News from spreading. But, those of them, and of us, who have been justified by faith, rejoice. Let us put aside any idols in our lives, and bow only before the One who saves us.

❧Day 17❧

Day
Verse: *For God so loved the world, that he gave his only begotten Son, that whosoever believeth in him should not perish, but have everlasting life.* **John 3:16**

Inspiration: Everybody knows this verse: God sent His son to earth for us. He died so that we may live. Believe in Him and you shall live forever. Blessed is the Lord!

Prayer: I do not deserve all that you have done for me, my loving and merciful Father. Forgive me for doubting, forgive me for selfishly wanting, forgive me for committing acts of hate, forgive me for forgetting my life's true purpose: to love you and spread your holy word. I love you God, and must help others do the same, as you did when you sent your son, Jesus Christ, to save us. In his name I pray. Amen.

❧Night❧

Verse: *For the grace of God that bring salvation hath appeared to all men, Teaching us that, denying ungodliness and worldly lusts, we should live soberly, righteously, and godly, in this present world;* **Titus 2:11-12**

Inspiration: As Christians, we know of the grace that God has shared with us freely so that we may be able to overcome sin. We have a part to play too, in taking action where need be. God has given us all we need to live uprightly, but it is our responsibility to live it out. Godliness should always be our standard.

Prayer: Dear God, I ask that you help me to always act in the right manner. Father, I desire to be godly in all my ways and I know that you have given me all I need in order to do so. Lord, may you help me in times where it seems like I am straying; guide me back to your way, Lord. In Jesus' name, I pray. Amen.

Devotion
Preparing the way

John the Baptist had the task of preparing the way for Jesus. If you remember the story of the sewer and the seed, you will remember that the seed that took root and flourished was the seed that landed on good ground. John's job was to till the soil of the people's hearts and bring them to repentance, so that they would be "good soil" for the seeds of the Good News that Jesus would bring. Even when people asked him if he was the Messiah, he denied it and pointed the way to Jesus. During the Passover Seder, the Jewish families will leave an empty place at the table for Elijah and if a person knocks on the door during the meal, they will invite that person in just in case he is Elijah. They are still waiting for the Messiah, and, by extension, they are still waiting for Elijah. Because they want to keep the promise of the covenant in the minds of their children, they also repeat the Exodus story each Passover. They want to make sure that the seed is good. We need to make sure that our soil and the soil of our children is also good and fertile and will welcome the seeds of faith. At this time of year, we have the perfect opportunity to do this by telling the story of Christmas and also the story of Jesus' life, death and resurrection. Perhaps the youngest child able to read could read the story of Jesus' birth from the Bible. What we read aloud stays in the mind longer than a story read by another. We also need to nurture that seed by sharing our experience of Jesus in our own lives; how our faith is important to us and brings us joy. Just like John, we too are asked to prepare the way for the Lord.

❧Day 18❧

Day

Verse: *For God so loved the world, that he gave his only begotten Son, that whosoever believeth in him should not perish, but have everlasting life.* **John 3:16**

Inspiration: The greatest gift we ever received was God's son, Jesus Christ. God loved us, in all of our ugliness and sin, so much that He willingly offered His son as a sacrificial lamb. We did nothing to deserve this gift and we cannot do anything to earn. We simply have to believe in Jesus and we receive the precious gift of everlasting life.

Prayer: Dear God, help me not to disrespect your gift or to fail to see what a sacrifice you made for me. When I was a sinner, you sent your son to save my soul for eternity. I am unworthy of this kind of love, but you gave it to me freely. I bow before you, O Lord. May I live a life that honors your sacrifice and draws others to you! In Jesus' name, Amen!

❧Night❧

Verse: *And he said to them all, if any man will come after me, let him deny himself, and take up his cross daily, and follow me.* **Luke 9:23**

Inspiration: We have sacrifices that we need to make to, as we choose to follow Christ. There are many worldly activities we have to give up, as they are not in line with what God has ordained us to do. Sometimes we have to leave certain friendships or relationships because they end up trying to pull us away from Christ. The joy in these sacrifices is that God always acknowledges them and they won't go unrewarded.

Prayer: Dear God, I acknowledge that there are things in my life that I may have to let go of as a result of my choosing to follow your way. Lord, I ask that you give me the strength I need to be able to let go, and may you comfort me in any time I feel pain. I thank you, Lord, that there is a greater glory ahead, that makes these sacrifices worthwhile. In Jesus' name, I pray. Amen.

Devotion
Blessed are they who do no evil

This passage from Isaiah is pretty much the same as what John the Baptist was telling the people as he preached his message of repentance and welcomed them to be baptized. This is just as relevant today as it was then. We are always in need of a reminder to repent of our sinfulness. We have one more week before we will celebrate Christmas. This is a reminder of what we need to do to be ready.

This time of year does bring out a spirit of generosity and most people say that they would love to see this spirit take root and be with us all year. However the reality is that it is usually gone before our New Year's resolutions are history.

We are asked to maintain a sense of justice year round. We are asked to do the right thing and refrain from doing evil. It is often difficult to keep a Sabbath because people are made to work so much that they have little time left for God. For many people, their day off is in the middle of the week and that's when they do everything they didn't do the rest of the week: laundry, cleaning, shopping, etc.

Where is the time for God? For the Jews, the Sabbath is Saturday and Orthodox Jews keep it. They don't drive or use electricity. In Israel, elevators stop on each floor automatically so that they don't even have to push buttons. Most Christians celebrate the Sabbath on the first day of the week instead of the seventh because Jesus rose from the dead on Sunday and they originally gathered to break bread on Sunday after going to the synagogue on Saturday.

Once they were kicked out of the synagogues, they just continued to meet on Sunday. Until fairly recently, Sunday was a day of church and rest but today, anything goes. If our lives have gotten too busy, to give God his due on Sunday, we need to choose another day that becomes our Sabbath. It is still important to give thanks and praise to God when we can.

❧Day 19❧

Day
Verse

For God sent not his Son into the world to condemn the world; but that the world through him might be saved.
John 3:17

Inspiration: It is amazing to think that Jesus came to this earth and lived among the sinners, but he did not come to condemn them. Instead, Jesus ate with the sinners. He loved them. He gave them an opportunity to escape their lives of sin and be saved and set free. While God is holy and could have sent his son to send all sinners to their deaths – he did the opposite. He gave them the gift of eternal life.

Prayer: Dear God, thank you for sending your son, Jesus Christ, not to condemn us before to offer us the gift of salvation. You are the Alpha and Omega, the Beginning and the End. It is within your power to destroy sin and sinner, but you extended your mercy. Because of Your love and sacrifice, we may live eternally. Thank you, O Lord. In Jesus' name, amen.

Night

Verse: *O magnifies the LORD with me, and let us exalt his name together.* **Psalm 34:3**

Inspiration: There is power in corporate praise and worship. When we come together as Christians to praise God together, we strengthen one another and we help one another to endure and push through the different challenges that we face. Don't shy away from your fellow brothers and sisters in Christ. Take time to meet together, pray together, and praise God.

Prayer: Dear God, I am grateful for my fellow brothers and sisters in Christ. I thank you, Lord, that whenever we gather, we get to experience your presence in such an awesome way. Father, I pray that the bond within the body of Christ will always be one of love and nothing else. In Jesus' name, I pray. Amen.

Devotion
Write your own devotion below!

❧Day 20❧

Day
Verse: *For I am persuaded, that neither death, nor life, nor angels, nor principalities, nor powers, nor things present, nor things to come, nor height, nor depth, nor any other creature, shall be able to separate us from the love of God, which is in Christ Jesus our Lord.* **Romans 8:38-39**

Inspiration: What is the farthest that you went out of love? Love can make us do things that we wouldn't normally do, but hurdles like distance, time, and effort can make even strong love crumble. What about the love of Jesus Christ? Not even DEATH was able to take that from us! Nothing can and nothing ever will. Believe this and we too can live a life free from fear, fear of judgment, fear of death.

Prayer: God, nothing can separate me from your love! I am so thankful for the strength and passion that instill in me, inciting courage within that I must share. I ask that you use me as a tool for good, so that I can bring others to see your love as I do. I ask all of this in accordance with your desires, my loving and powerful creator. Amen.

❧Night❧

Verse: *Many are the afflictions of the righteous: but the LORD delivered him out of them all. He keeps all his bones: not one of them is broken.*
Psalm 34:19-20

Inspiration: As Christians we should always keep in mind that we could face persecution, mockery, beatings, isolation, and attacks for being advocates of the gospel. But we should also remember that these moments of affliction will never gain any comparison to the glory of what is to come on the day of the Resurrection, where we will receive new glorious bodies, free from infirmities and sin. It is because of this, we gladly go through all we go through, because we know that everything we face on this earth is temporary.

Prayer: Dear God, I am aware of what may come my way because I choose to align myself with you. I do not consider it any loss, the suffering I may endure on this earth, as a result of my faith in you. Whatever my earthly body endures on this earth, as a result of being a Christian, I count it worth it when I think of the glory that is to come. In Jesus' name, I pray. Amen.

Devotion
It has been revealed, proclaim it

This is the last Sunday before Christmas and today we hear Paul give God the glory due him for sending his Son as the fulfillment of the covenant first proclaimed to Abraham, and declared by all the prophets, especially Isaiah whom we have been listening to during this season, and will continue to do on Christmas. Now, Paul is telling the new Christians in Rome the "Good News" of Jesus' coming and his preaching which declared the promise of eternal life and the path he has given us to follow. How have we done this Advent to prepare for the commemoration of Jesus' birth? Have we been distracted by the world's pressure to spend money on what will only bring a temporary pleasure, or have we spent time with the Lord? Have we been more generous with our time, and helped those whose needs were greater than our own? Have we taught our children to give and not just receive? Will we reach out to those who are alone or lonely and invite them to celebrate with us? What have we done or do we plan to do to make this Christmas a true celebration of Christ? Are we more ready to meet Jesus when he comes again? One Christmas morning I was in church and the presided told the story of his grandfather. It was the grandfather's tradition to tell the story of his childhood where there was little money and so each child received an orange for a gift. He wanted to enjoy this gift for more than a few minutes and so he would only eat one segment of the orange a day until it was gone.

When it was time to gather for dinner, he didn't come to the table. God had called him home. He was ready. Would we, would I be?

❧Day 21❧

Day

Verse: *And the Word was made flesh, and dwelt among us, (and we beheld his glory, the glory as of the only begotten of the Father,) full of grace and truth.* **John 1:14**

Inspiration: Jesus, the Word of God, was sent to earth as a baby to live as a man. He grew from a baby in the womb to the Savior on the cross. He lived among us, He ate with us, and He healed us. By taking on flesh, He also took on our sins on the cross. His death on the cross is what granted us reconciliation with his father. May we never forget His sacrifice!

Prayer: Dear God, You sent your son to this fallen world to offer us atonement when we did not deserve it. Thank you for your mercy and grace, O Lord. You sent the holy word down to our world full of sin to shine like a light in the darkness. Knowing we are children of God, may we live like Your Son, Jesus Christ. In His precious name, amen!

❧Night❧

Verse: *For though we walk in the flesh, we do not war after the flesh:(For the weapons of our warfare are not carnal, but mighty through God to the pulling down of strong holds; Casting down imaginations, and every high thing that exalted itself against the knowledge of God, and bringing into captivity every thought to the obedience of Christ;* **2 Corinthians 10:3-5**

Inspiration: As Christians, we need to remember that the battles we face are not physical. Every form of opposition be it in man or in circumstances, though it may come in the physical, is actually spiritual. Attacks will come in the form of people and strenuous situations but we cannot afford to not see everything as spiritual. God has equipped us and He covers us to ensure that the enemy will never overthrow us, no matter what.

Prayer: Dear God, I am aware that, every day, the enemy tries to attack me through the words and actions of people and through stressful situations too. Father, in times where the fight may seem like too much, I ask that you help me stand firm on your word. May I never forget that I already have the victory! In Jesus' name, I pray. Amen.

By ALM Projects

Devotion
God us with us

The Lord, your God, is among you. Think about it. God is in our midst. This is a true statement today, just as it was when Jesus walked the earth and when God was among the Israelites in the desert and in all their trials. Do we recognize God's presence? We won't recognize God presence unless we look for it. Where should we be looking? First, we should be looking in the mirror! If we believe that we are made in the image and likeness of God, than we are the living face of God. And so is everyone else we meet? So the second place we need to look is at the faces around us during the day. That includes family, friends, neighbors, co-workers, and people we don't even know but pass along the way. Then we look at the beauty of creation and actually see it, not just take it for granted. The sun, the flowers, the clouds, even the rain are the works of God. Did anything happen today that made you smile? Thank God. Did you get through a tough time at home or at work? Thank God. Just a few more days until Christmas! Relax and enjoy the spirit of joy around you. If you haven't had the time or money to celebrate the way you would like, don't worry about it! Stress is not joy and God wants us to rejoice. When I was a child, I knew that we weren't as well off as others, but I never thought about what we didn't have only what we had. I know it's more difficult today because the ads tell us what we should have! Sorry, there is no what that I would buy any of those expensive toys even if I did have the money. And the most important gift is Jesus. Love is the greatest gift we can give our children

114

and it's what will matter in the long run. God is in our midst; let us rejoice.

❧Day 22❧

Day
Verse: *And so it was, that, while they were there, the days were accomplished that she should be delivered. And she brought forth her firstborn son, and wrapped him in swaddling clothes, and laid him in a manger; because there was no room for them in the inn.* **Luke 2:6-7**

Inspiration: We return to the figure of the baby Jesus here, not draped in golden cloth, delivered within a palace to fanfare, but birthed at an inn, amongst the animals, emerging into this world a humble Son not above the majority of men. Jesus not only preached a gospel of venerating the lowly, the underprivileged, the plebian, but He Himself practiced it, living amongst them. Could we do the same? Could we celebrate God's glory outside of the comfort of our current social strata or privileges?

Prayer: Divine Glory and Love Everlasting, in Jesus' name I pray. Lord makes me more perfect each day, in the image of Your Son. Help me cast off what is not needed in my life, and instead show me what is truly important. Let me not show contempt or condemnation for any of Your children, no matter their status, for I know that we may all be Your prodigal sons and daughters, sinful and mistaken, but still nevertheless, loved and forgiven. Amen.

❧Night ❧

Verse: *Come unto me, all ye that labor and are heavy laden, and I will give you rest. Take my yoke upon you, and learn of me; for I am meek and lowly in heart: and ye shall find rest unto your souls. For my yoke is easy, and my burden is light.* **Matthew 11:28-30**

Inspiration: Are you tired of trying to overcome sin on your own? Are you worn out from trying to be perfect, in your own power? Have you tried to be righteous on your own and found yourself seriously wanting? Here is the good news: you don't have to do this on your own. Jesus Christ paid the price for us, so that we could be saved from our sin, and so that we could also be partakers of the Father's inheritance. The life of Christ is an unburdened life, filled with rest and blessed assurance.

Prayer: Dear God, I thank you for the rest and peace I have in you as a result of what your son, Jesus Christ, did for me. Lord, I have struggled with my sin and I have grown weary from trying to be perfect on my own. Thank you, Father, for removing the burden from my shoulders and helping me overcome my struggles. In Jesus' name, I pray. Amen

Devotion
Finding God in the unexpected

When the Magi visited Herod looking for the child who would be king, this is the prophecy that his advisors found that sent them on to Bethlehem to find Jesus. Bethlehem was a small town, but it was the place of David's birth and so, being of the house and family of David, Mary and Joseph needed to go to Bethlehem for the census. And now another King would be born there! Without this prophecy, would anyone think that a king would come from there? I'm sure people thought that a great ruler should come from a great place like Jerusalem. Maybe we have some of those hidden prejudices. How do we judge others? I know and you know that we shouldn't judge, but sometimes we have prejudices that we are unaware of. At one time or another, I have been a waitress, a door to door salesperson, a teacher, a cashier, and a clerk in a business office. I have had to learn many different skills in order to do these jobs. And I have developed expectations of others who do these jobs. I try very hard when I encounter a person in any one of these professions to do their jobs correctly. Sometimes when I encounter a person who does a poor job, I have to remind myself that I am not the one who signs their paycheck and it's not my job to judge them. When Jesus began his ministry, he was once again put down for coming from Nazareth, another small town with nothing to recommend it. So, we can at times judge people for the skills we think they should have, or where they come from, or how well they speak, or for a hundred other reasons and we don't even realize we are doing it. Would we have given Jesus a chance, or would we have judged him by his origins? Interesting question as we prepare again for his coming.

❧Day 23❧

Day

Verse: *Therefore if any man be in Christ, he is a new creature: old things are passed away; behold all things are become new.* **2 Corinthians 5:17**

Inspiration: You might often wish yourself to be someone else, but so often it is easy to forget your own value when comparing yourself to others who seem perhaps far richer, more successful, popular, or happy. The simple truth is that we do not really know what dwells within others' hearts, for our envy of them more often than not consists of our own projections, largely of our own selfish making. If we seek to be someone else, someone new, think back to John's baptism, or of the prodigal son returning home. We cannot escape ourselves, but in Him, in our faith, there are ways in which we may be remade in his image. By having the Lord show us infinite mercy, and forgiving us all our sins, we are purged of the old, and we may thus be made anew each and every day, in the eyes of the Lord.

Prayer: Lord God in Heaven above re-makes me into your image, with a heart that is clean. Cast off my past transgressions, and wash my body clean of all things passed away and which I cannot change. I ask all this Lord, so that I may be made anew, my heart eager to love and serve You, Amen.

❧Night❧

Verse: *Now unto him that is able to do exceeding abundantly above all that we ask or think, according to the power that worked in us, unto him be glory in the church by Christ Jesus throughout all ages, world without end. Amen.* **Ephesians 3:20-21**

Inspiration

God really is able to do far more than you can imagine or desire in your life. He is the God of all things good and pure, and He is your Father. Knowing this should give you confidence when you pray and when you are in times of need. It doesn't matter how impossible the situation may appear to be; God will always provide for you. That will never change.

Prayer: Dear God, I thank you that I never have to worry about lacking a thing because you are always there for me. Lord, even when the situation may appear to be far beyond saving, I know that you will always make a way; your word tells me so. When I feel discouraged, may I find comfort in you, Lord. In Jesus' name, I pray. Amen.

Devotion
Behold he comes

We're getting closer! I'm sure the prophecies we've been reading the past few days are the same ones that Jesus mentioned to the disciples on the road to Emmaus, and have been examined over the years, as those that point to the Messiah. Malachi is not one of the Major Prophets, and this book is placed last in the Old Testament. He is upset that they Israelites upon returning from exile pick up where they left off with abuses by their leaders as well as by the people. They are impatient for the Messiah to appear. So Malachi gives us this prophecy which lets the people know that the Lord, whom they seek will appear. First, John, the messenger, comes to prepare the way, and then Jesus appears in the temple. John is the last prophet of the first covenant, and Jesus brings us the new. There was a time when people thought that we didn't need the Old Testament, the old covenant, just the New Testament. But wiser heads prevailed! How could we understand the New without the Old. Jesus himself said that he had not come to abolish the law – the first covenant – but to fulfill it. This means that we can't just throw out the old. How else would we know of Abraham or Moses, King David and Solomon, the prophets or the times they were faithful and the times they went astray and needed God to save them. All of this is important for us, as we also are sometimes faithful and sometimes we need saving from ourselves. We learn from both the old and the new and are called to follow Jesus, as he followed the teachings of the Law.

❧Day 24❧

Day

Verse: *There hath no temptation taken you but such as is common to man: but God is faithful, who will not suffer you to be tempted above that ye are able; but will with the temptation also make a way to escape, that ye may be able to bear it.* **1 Corinthians 10:13**

Inspiration: Though God sends trials and allows temptations to enter our lives, He is ever near and ready to help. He is faithful to help us through everything we face. He will provide a way to escape temptations and a way to endure hardships if we will but take it.

Prayer: May I not make excuses or try to blame you for my failings or resent trials or discipline you send into my life. Help me to see each test as an opportunity to choose you and to die the more to self. Trusting in Your Spirit working in me to will and do of your good pleasure, may I find the strength, will, and wisdom to reject sin and choose God.

❧Night❧

Verse: *But while he thought on these things, behold, the angel of the Lord appeared unto him in a dream, saying, Joseph, thou son of David, fear not to take unto thee Mary thy wife: for that which is conceived in her is of the Holy Ghost.* **Matthew 1:20**

Inspiration: When we are walking in God's path, God will always confirm His word to the people in our lives who need to know. After God had given Mary instructions, and she'd become pregnant via the Holy Spirit, He sent an angel to assure Joseph of His plans. This stopped Joseph from divorcing Mary. Don't be worried, when you follow the instructions of God in your life. He will take care of everything else.

Prayer: Dear God, I thank you that when it comes to following your way, I have nothing to worry about because you have taken care of anything. I know that your word will be confirmed, no matter who may or may not believe it in my life. Because of this, I choose to move forward in the path you have set out for me. In Jesus' name, I pray. Amen.

Devotion
Joseph the unsung hero

We haven't thought about Joseph's role in salvation yet. Joseph must have been very confused when he found out that Mary was pregnant, but because he loved her, he didn't want her to be disgraced and possible stoned to death. He believed the angel, married Mary, and became the foster father of Jesus. No one knew that he wasn't actually Jesus' father. There are so many men who take on the responsibility of being father to another man's son or daughter. I have watched my own son over the years be father to his stepson. He could not love his own child more, and has always treated him with as much love as he does his two daughters. He is not alone. What makes a child a son or daughter? I believe that it is love. Joseph loved Jesus and raised him to be a faithful Jewish boy, brought him to the synagogue so that he would know the Scriptures and taught him the skills of being a carpenter. He gives us an example of what it means to be a parent regardless of the circumstances. My son is not alone in step-parenting or adoption. There have been people who have fostered or adopted children who have special needs or who have been abandoned by their parents, or who have lost their parents to death or drugs. As long as we love, we can welcome another person into our hearts and into our families. When asked how many grandchildren I have, I always include this very special addition to our family and was never prouder than when he called me "Nana" for the first time. I'm sure that Joseph felt the same when Jesus called him "Abba."

❧Day 25❧

Day

Verse: *We are bound to thank God always for you, brethren, as it is meet, because that your faith growth exceedingly, and the charity of every one of you all toward each other abounded;* 2 **Thessalonians 1-3**

Inspiration: The Christian life was not designed to be lived alone, so we should show our thankfulness and love for one another. Showing love to others is a true outward expression of our faith in Christ and how He loved us. Therefore, as we grow in our faith, our love for others should also increase. When we begin to understand Christ's sacrifice more fully, we will be more willing to give of ourselves to others.

Prayer: Dear God, thank you for sending your son, Jesus Christ, to not only die for our sins, but to also show us how to love others unselfishly. Please surround me with people who love me and that I love so we may more fully understand your sacrifice and grow closer to you. Help me to live a life modeled after the way You love, O Lord. In Jesus' name, amen.

❧Night❧

Verse: *For God sent not his Son into the world to condemn the world; but that the world through him might be saved.* **John 3:17**

Inspiration: God did not send His son to condemn us. God did the total opposite – He sent His son to save us from condemnation and eternal damnation. The reason why we can gladly say we are children of God, and that the salvation we have received is eternal, is because God gave His son up to pay the price so that we wouldn't have to. We will never find a love greater than this from anyone else.

Prayer: Dear God, I will always be in awe when I think of how great your love for me, and everyone in this world, is. We weren't anywhere close to righteous when you sent your Son, Jesus Christ, to die for us; but that did not stop you. It did not move you away from us. If anything, it compelled you even more to redeem us and you did this without anyone asking. You truly are a Good, Good, Father. In Jesus' name, I pray. Amen.

Devotion
Jesus our Savior is born, rejoice

Happy Christmas! I hope you have a wonderful day today, full of joy and blessings. For many of you it will be a work day because your job requires it. For others it is a work day because you may work with animals or crops and every day is a work day. But we rejoice because God loves us so much that he allowed his son to enter into humanity, to become one of us even though he is God, so that we could be saved. The kingdom he established is still rooted on this earth in us who believe and who carry on the mission that he gave us. Even though it will only reach its completion in the afterlife, it is evolving because we continue to love one another and work for justice in order to help "God's kingdom come on earth as it is in heaven." Take some time today to sit and ponder what this birth has meant in your life. If you have children, read the story of the birth of Jesus in Luke and in Matthew. Let them know the importance of the day; that it is not just a day of gifts and food, but the celebration of a life that will give them eternal life. Give thanks to God for all you have and let them give thanks for something that is important to them. Sing a Christmas carol or two, and if you have small children, let them sing "Happy Birthday" to Jesus. Unless we pass on the truth of Christmas, how are they to know?

❧Day 26❧

Day

Verse: *There is no fear in love; but perfect love casted out fear: because fear hath torment. He that feared is not made perfect in love.* **John4:18**

Inspiration: Perhaps our greatest fears in love are tied up with that of rejection, or of our partners being unfaithful. These fears may torment us, and often as a result negatively affect our relationships as our torments transform into paranoia, suspicions, and isolation. These are all understandable attempts at self-preservation, to keep oneself from being vulnerable and hurt, but ultimately they result in also destroying everything. In matters of the spirit, we must remain resolute in

God, faithful in His promise never to leave or abandon us. In matters of our Lord, we must keep our hearts free from fear, for in Him we have found a lasting partner and merciful Father.

Prayer: Lord and Heavenly Father, whose house has many mansions, I pray for you to keep me from fear. Take my darkness, my insecurities and suspicions, and show them the light of your truth, which never leaves us. Strengthen my trust in your love. I ask this so I may be thy perfect partner and servant, blessed in everlasting love, Amen.

❧Night❧

Verse: *And Joseph also went up from Galilee, out of the city of Nazareth, into Judaea, unto the city of David, which is called Bethlehem; (because* *he was of the house and lineage of David :) To be taxed with Mary his espoused wife, being great with child.* **Luke 2:4-5**

Inspiration: It's amazing to think that the son of God came from a family that appeared to be so normal – a carpenter and his wife. Jesus' birth was also not what one would have expected for the son of God. He was born in a manger. But look at what came from Him. He grew to be Jesus Christ, and He fulfilled the Scriptures. We have eternal life because of this Savior, who did not appear to be one to the people around Him. Thank God for the knowledge and understanding you have of who Jesus Christ is.

Prayer: Dear God, I am grateful that I have come to an understanding on who you are and who your son, Jesus Christ is. Lord, to anyone in those times they may not have realized what was happening, but I am grateful that I have become a partaker of that sacrifice that happened all those years ago. In Jesus' name, I pray. Amen.

Devotion
We must keep the faith

Stephen was one of the first deacons, and is considered the first Christian martyr. He spoke boldly of Jesus and the Good News of the coming of the Kingdom. The same leaders who hated Jesus, and couldn't contain the apostles, now hated Stephen and worked up the crowd to the point of frenzy. The crowd attacked Stephen and stoned him to death. The story of the stoning of Stephen also introduces us to a young Jewish man named Saul who persecuted the Christians until his experience of Jesus changes him and he becomes Paul, the Apostle to the Gentiles. Stephen's story lets us know that it is not easy to be a Christian witness. It takes courage today in the face of the world's rejection of Gospel values as well as the rise of atheism. I have not encountered such a rejection of a belief in God as I do today. Most of the world believes in someone or something greater than themselves. Whether we call God Lord, Allah, Yahweh, or Jehovah, we are calling on the one God, even if we have different understandings of who God is. Other cultures such as Hinduism and Zoroastrianism, still believe in the gods of their religions. But atheism denies the existence of any god. To talk about Christianity in this environment and to work for its ideals, is very counter-cultural and takes courage. Stephen was willing to risk everything for Christ. Are you, am I, willing to risk ridicule for our values? Will we stand by when we see injustice or will be stand up for justice for everyone? We have choices, just as Stephen did; may we have his courage and confidence in the promises of Christ.

❧Day 27❧

Day

Verse: *But sanctify the Lord God in your hearts: and be ready always to give an answer to every man that asked you a reason of the hope that is in you with meekness and fear:* **1 Peter 3:15**

Inspiration: To those who know nothing of God's love, it may seem quite unintuitive how someone might devote themselves to the Lord. The better we know and understand these ourselves, the better may we provide an answer to these questions from others! Look deep within yourself to find these answers, or consult with your ministers. Questions are not like plagues, to be avoided at all costs.

They are how we find our truth; do not shirk them, but welcome them.

Prayer: God Almighty my redeemer and salvation, grant me strength to search in your light for the truth. I may not always be certain, and doubts may sometimes plague my mind, but grant me the fortitude to march forward in your name, spreading truth amongst those who have not yet accepted You into their hearts. **Amen.**

❧Night❧

Verse: *Therefore if any man be in Christ, he is a new creature: old things are passed away; behold all things are become new.* **2 Corinthians 5:17**

Inspiration: Human life ends. Life through Christ is endless. Who you are now does not mean that is who you have to be later. If we submit to the Lord and believe, we can change from something that ends to something eternal.

Prayer: I want to be closer to you, O Lord, my God. Give me the courage to follow your word and believe in all the good that you have given to those of us that struggle to comprehend. Help me to comprehend and I will live everyday like that gift that it is. I will do this as your son, Jesus Christ, showed me, and it is in his name that I pray. Amen.

Devotion
Finding Sanctuary

Joseph was warned that Jesus was in danger and fled to Egypt so that they would be safe. It's a good thing that this wasn't today because they had no papers, no passport, and no visa. It is getting increasingly difficult to find sanctuary in a world that looks at anyone from another part of the world with suspicion. It couldn't have been easy for Joseph or Mary. Would they be welcome? Would Joseph be able to support his young family? Would Mary find a safe environment in which to raise this very special son? So many families today must make choices about where they can live and how they can be safe. I once worked with a woman who was married to a man who had escaped from the country of his birth in order to save his life. Men of his age were conscripted into the army of the dictator and he knew he would never survive because he wouldn't be able to rape and kill. He could only stay in this country because they were married. Men, women and children try to escape such conditions every day. Some are lucky enough to gain sanctuary, but too many others are turned away from the borders or killed in the attempt. People have drowned in oceans and seas because they have overfilled boats or rafts trying to get to freedom. Joseph was able to find a safe place for Mary and Jesus, may those who flee oppression find sanctuary in our world today.

❧Day 28❧

Day
Verse: *For he has made him to be sin for us, who knew no sin; that we might be made the righteousness of God in him.* **2 Corinthians**

Inspiration: Jesus was sinless, yet God sent him to live in our sinful world among sinful men. Then, Jesus died on the cross for our sin. He was innocent, yet he was treated as though he was guilty. We were guilty, but through His sacrifice, we are seen as innocent. This transfer of righteousness through His death on the cross is more than we deserve.

Prayer: Dear God, You sent your son, Jesus Christ, to our undeserving world. We are sinners, but you took our place on the cross. You received our guilt and allowed us to share in your righteousness. Your mercy is more than I can comprehend. O Lord, thank you for loving us enough to make such a sacrifice for my redemption. Help me to live a life honoring this sacrifice. In Jesus' name, amen.

❧Night❧

Verse: *To wit, that God was in Christ, reconciling the world unto himself, not imputing their trespasses unto them; and hath committed unto us the word of reconciliation. Now then we are ambassadors for Christ, as though God did beseech you by us: we pray you in Christ's stead, be ye reconciled to God.* **2 Corinthians 5:19-20**

Inspiration: "We pray you in Christ's stead, be ye reconciled to God." Jesus died for us. He knew the experience that he would go through and did it so that we could be saved. Yet so many of us refuse to reconcile and commit to his word. We must. We must implore others to do the same. Through this, we will be saved.

Prayer: O merciful and forgiving God, implore me to seek you more. Help me to help others do the same. Through your words and deeds all that I need to know can be known. Forgive me for not always committing fully, and help me commit more in the future. I humbly ask all of this in your Holy name, my Lord. Amen.

Devotion
We must protect our children

Today is the feast of the Holy Innocents marking the slaughter of innocent children in an attempt to kill

Jesus! Many innocent children today die from preventable causes. No clean water or air, lack of adequate medical care, insufficient food and warfare are all reasons why children die. There is no reason for any of this to happen. The causes, however, are usually based on greed. Often warfare will cause some of the other causes of death to occur because of the amount of money the government spends on the military rather than on making sure that the people have the basic necessities of life. Other times, the government leaders just don't spend the money needed but build up their own bank accounts. There are many charitable organizations which work to dig wells, provide education as to how to purify the water, and train communities in basic medical care and nutrition, but some of these organizations have trouble getting permission from the government to do the work. One summer, I worked as a nanny for two children from Nigeria. Their father was in the United States to work on a project that was important to his company. As a committed Christian, he provided a medical and dental clinic on company property for all of his employees and their families. Although he was a Nigerian citizen and it was a Nigerian company, he said that he had to be very careful that these benefits did not imply that the government wasn't doing its job. Parents are often forced to leave their countries because of the wars waged between government forces and those who are fighting for change. The innocent still suffer and die. This is a good day to pray for all children that they may have the basic necessities of food, water, shelter, medical care and education as well as to ask God to help us know what we can do to be part of the solution.

❧Day 29❧

Day
Verse: *For the love of Christ constraints us; because we thus judge, that if one died for all, then were all dead: And that he died for all, that they which live should not henceforth live unto themselves, but unto him which died for them, and rose again.*
2 Corinthians 5:14-1

Inspiration: Jesus' sacrifice upon the cross truly shows us God's love for us. Would we ourselves be willing to ever do the same? God once tested Abraham to offer up his own son as a sacrifice in order to show his devotion. Could we have done the same? Does our love truly move so deeply within us for the Lord? God has proven himself too, for on the hills of

Golgotha He offered up His only Son to us. For even if we would falter imperfectly and fail to live up to Abraham's devotion, our Lord God cannot and will not fail in His love for us, His side of the covenant is complete.

Prayer: My God all merciful hallowed be your name! I come to ask for forgiveness and guidance. I am not perfect, with all fears and doubts, but I beg of you to give divine grace in your love and to extend this gift unto all of mankind. Renew my spirit Lord, so that I may give myself up in glorious devotion to your loving embrace, and may this bond never be broken. For I am servant, your sheep and your child, Amen.

❧Night☙

Verse: *Brethren, if a man be overtaken in a fault, ye which are spiritual, restore such an one in the spirit of meekness; considering thyself, lest thou also be tempted.* **Galatians 6:1**

Inspiration: I saw a story on the news of people forming a chain with their arms to save a child stuck in a river. Their thoughtless bravery ended up saving the child, but just thinks how easily they could have been swept away. Sin is not so different from a raging river, and the temptations are very real, as we all know. As with this story, with the right people around you and a clear goal in mind, even the strongest of rivers is no match for a faithful community.

Prayer: I am a sinner, my Lord. Forgive me for my weaknesses and help me to forgive the trespasses of others against me. These repressed thoughts are sins themselves, and I ask that you instill a calmness in my heart, knowing that you will always be there for me. Your grace will never be forgotten, my Lord, nor the sacrifices of your son to absolve me of my sins. Amen.

Devotion
Walk in the light of the lord

And so the question is, do we want to walk in darkness or in the light? One of my favorite hymns is "I Want to Walk as a Child of the Light." The opening line continues, "I want to follow Jesus." Although the hymn is primarily directed at children, it should say something to us as well. Walking in the light means following Jesus and living out his commandment of love. The dark hides so much while the light allows us to see everything. If we walk in the light, we allow ourselves to look honestly at our behavior and shine a light into all the corners. Are there some habits we have gotten into that we don't think of as sinful? I know that there are those who would be shocked to find out that their language is actually sinful – swearing and cursing, breaking the commandment to not take the name of the Lord in vain. Do we realize that gossip, even if what we say is true, can kill a person's reputation, lose them a job, or ruin a relationship? The other day, I was attempting to cross the street in a crosswalk, with a walk light, and three cars ran right through the light. I guess they believed that they were more important than my safety. And we know that this happens every day with people hurt and killed as a result. Do they realize that this is a sin? If we are serious about walking in the light and following Jesus, these are but some of the things we need to think about. I'm sure that you can think of other things that are traps we fall into thinking that it doesn't matter because everyone does it. Let's not kid ourselves and promise to do a better job at allowing the light to shine in so that we truly are following Jesus.

❧Day 30❧

Day

Verse: *I beseech you therefore, brethren, by the mercies of God, that ye present your bodies a living sacrifice, holy, acceptable unto God, which is your reasonable service.* **Romans 12:1**

Inspiration: Although God may call some of His children to make the ultimate sacrifice as martyrs, most of us He calls to a life of service and self-denial. We are to be a "living sacrifice," offered to God fully but to live for Him rather than die. And this, Paul tells us, is but our "reasonable service," not some above and beyond call to "extra" service.

Prayer: Help me, O Lord, to live every day, hour, and moment fully for You, not simply pursuing my own selfish desires. May I not count it unreasonable to serve You with all of my life. May I not grumble and complain over things sacrificed for the sake of Your Kingdom, but surrender all things joyfully that You may require.

❧Night❧

Verse: I will love thee, O LORD, my strength. The LORD is my rock, and my fortress, and my deliverer; my God, my strength, in whom I will trust; my buckler, and the horn of my salvation, and my high tower. **Psalm 18:1-2**

Inspiration: God is always there for us, when we need him or not, but I think the most important part of this verse is the beginning. How often do we say and feel that we truly love God? Often we use him simply as our rock, our refuge, or our strength. When times are good, we often neglect to remember him. So go, love the Lord, the people, and leave everything else to God.

Prayer: Dear heavenly Father, the truest love of my life, thank you for always being there for me. Forgive me, my Lord, for seeking you only when I need strength and support, and help me realize how fortunate I am that you are still always there. I wish to be more like you in my ways Lord, and be the strength for those around me as well. I pray to my rock and redeemer, my love and my Lord. Amen.

Devotion

Knowing Jesus means keeping the commandments

From the days of Moses at Mount Sinai, the consistent theme of how we know God is to keep his commandments. It was true then and it is true today. If we know God, we keep his commandments. Yesterday we talked about the sins we may not even realize we are committing, but today we need to take a closer look at the commandments. It's not surprising that keeping the first commandment of believing in one God and not having any other gods before him is taken for granted, but! From Adam and Eve to us, the temptation to be in control of our lives is alive and well. We don't need to even think about original sin: we want to be God. No? Well, the serpent told Eve that the reason God didn't want them to eat of the fruit of the tree of the knowledge of good and evil was because if they did, they would be like him – and they wanted to be like him. God wants us to obey rules that are made to help us; we hate to be told what to do. One of the first words a toddler learns is "no." We may not kill, but we hold onto anger, and violence is a response for many people to situations where they don't get what they want. Fidelity in marriage is not considered a priority for many people and the media exploits this with programs that actively encourage sexual behavior as "fun" and no strings attached! Vandalism, as well as plagiarism is rampant. Scandals concerning educational qualifications and work applications are common. Do people understand that this too is theft? Truth can be hard to find in personal relationships, work ethics and the political arena. We want what everyone else has which leads to envy and often destructive behavior. We need to know the commandments in our hearts as well as in our minds. Then we need to keep them.

❧Day 31❧

Day

Verse: *But ye are a chosen generation, a royal priesthood, an holy nation, a peculiar people; that ye should show forth the praises of him who hath called you out of darkness into his marvelous light:* **1 Peter 2:9**

Inspiration: Have you ever stopped to consider that God chose you? The Bible tells us we are a chosen generation, a royal priesthood, a holy nation, a peculiar people – we should not look upon this lightly. We have a calling because the Lord called us out of the darkness. We get to run into his marvelous light as we have been set free from the captivity of sin and darkness. The God of the Universe calls you chosen – praise His name!

Prayer: Dear God, I am humbled by your majesty and Your willingness to allow me to enter into Your kingdom. You have saved me from the darkness and welcomed me into the light. Help me to live my life as one of your chosen people. May I live my life as one who knows I am a considered a child of the holiest god. Help me to shine in the light of your glory so others may see you. In Jesus' name, amen.

❧Night☙

Verse: *Herein is love, not that we loved God, but that he loved us, and sent his Son to be the propitiation for our sins.* **1 John 4:10**

Inspiration: Love did not begin with man. It is not a worldly human creation. It is a divine creation. Love came from God to us, not the other way around. This loving action gave us the opportunity to reciprocate this action to God and to others. In **1 John 4:9, John** explains that Jesus was sent to us as an act of love, to show us the meaning. Live according to God's love and we do not need to fear judgment, living and loving freely and truthfully.

Prayer

Faithful and righteous God, forgive me for not always living according to your edicts. I know that you sent your son to earth as an act of love, one that I can never repay, but I ask that you help me honor this act of love through my own loving actions. I am inspired to be more like Jesus and more like you, heavenly Father, to honor the love you have for me. I pray this in your holy name. Amen.

Devotion
Give me a spirit of righteousness

Today is the last day of the calendar year. What a great time to look back over the year and see how well – or not – we have followed the Lord. In the course of a year, we follow the life of Jesus from the moment of his conception to his birth, and his public life which led to his death and resurrection. In some ways, it's too bad that the calendar year and what is called "the liturgical year," don't coincide. So we end the year with the celebration of Jesus birth, spring brings his death and resurrection and the summer has most of his public life! But the timing really doesn't matter; what matters is the looking forward to his return and also looking back at the year we just lived and examine our progress in faith. Over the past year, how did God answer your prayers? When did you experience God in the joyous moments? How did you experience God's help when you called upon him? When did God show you his forgiveness? When did he help you to forgive? Recalling all of these experiences, and more, will help to give us a firmer resolve to do even better in the year to come. This also might be a good time to think about our actions that might have caused another person pain. It is difficult to avoid hurting people, especially those whom we love, because they expect more from us. The hurt is often unintentional, but it's there and we often don't even realize what we've done. More than once, someone has promised to do something and then promptly forgot. I bet I have done the same. As the year ends, I need to ask forgiveness and if that's not possible, then I need to pray for those whom I have hurt. What about you?

DECEMBER WITH GOD
                              By ALM Projects

172